CARB COUNTING

A straightforward guidebook on

the techniques of carb-counting

for diabetes and weight loss for

beginners

SARA GRISHAM

Table of Contents

CHAPTER ONE

INTRODUCTION

Nutrition and physical activity are important parts of a healthy lifestyle when you have diabetes. Along with other benefits, following a healthy meal plan and being active can help you keep your blood glucose level, also called blood sugar, in your target range. To manage your blood glucose, you need to balance what you eat and drink with physical activity and diabetes medicine if you take any. What you choose to

4

eat, how much you eat, and when you eat are all important in keeping your blood glucose level in the range that your healthcare team recommends. Becoming more active and making changes in what you eat and drink can seem challenging at first. You may find it easier to start with small changes and get help from your family, friends, and healthcare team.

Eating well and being physically active most days of the week can help you

- keep your blood glucose level, blood pressure, and cholesterol in your target ranges
- lose weight or stay at a healthy weight
- prevent or delay diabetes problems
- feel good and have more energy

WHAT FOODS CAN I EAT IF I HAVE DIABETES?

You may worry that having diabetes means going without foods you enjoy. The good news is that you can still eat your favorite foods, but you might need to eat smaller portions or enjoy them less often. Your healthcare team will help create a diabetes meal plan for you that meets your needs and likes.

The key to eating with diabetes is to eat a variety of healthy foods from all food groups, in the amounts your meal plan outlines.

THE FOOD GROUPS ARE

- vegetables
- nonstarchy: includes broccoli, carrots, greens, peppers, and tomatoes

- starchy: includes potatoes, corn, and green peas
- fruits—includes oranges, melon, berries, apples, bananas, and grapes
- grains—at least half of your grains for the day should be whole grains
- Includes wheat, rice, oats, cornmeal, barley, and quinoa
- Examples: bread, pasta, cereal, and tortillas
- protein
- lean meat

- chicken or turkey without the skin
- fish
- eggs
- nuts and peanuts
- dried beans and certain peas, such as chickpeas and split peas
- meat substitutes, such as tofu
- dairy—nonfat or low fat
- milk or lactose-free milk if you have lactose intolerance
- yogurt
- cheese

Eat foods with heart-healthy fats, which mainly come from these foods:

- oils that are liquid at room temperatures, such as canola and olive oil
- nuts and seeds
- heart-healthy fish such as salmon, tuna, and mackerel
- avocado
- Use oils when cooking food instead of butter, cream, shortening, lard, or stick margarine.

WHAT TYPES OF FOOD AND BEVERAGES SHOULD I AVOID IF I HAVE DIABETES?

THINGS TO CONSIDER REDUCING ARE

fast food and other sources of saturated and trans fat foods rich in sodium, generally known as salt; sweets; beverages with added sugars; examples including juice, ordinary soda, and typical sports or energy drinks; and salt-free meals Replace sugary drinks with water. Think about switching to a sugar-free sweetener for your morning beverage.

You should limit your alcohol consumption to no more than one drink per day for women and no more than two drinks per day for men. Alcohol consumption increases the risk of hypoglycemia in those whose blood sugar is controlled by insulin or other diabetic medications that boost insulin production. If you haven't eaten in a while, this is especially true. Eating meals before consuming alcohol is recommended.

HOW OFTEN SHOULD I EAT IF I HAVE DIABETES?

To keep their blood sugar levels stable, some persons with diabetes must eat at around the same time every day. Others have greater leeway in terms of when they eat. If you have diabetes, you may need to take insulin or take your diabetic medication at the same time every day, and you may also need to consume the same quantity of carbs. Meal-time insulin allows you to eat whenever you choose.

Skipping or postponing a meal while taking insulin or another type of diabetic medication might cause dangerously low blood sugar levels. Find out if you need to eat before or after you exercise, and at what times, from your medical staff.

WHAT IS THE DIABETES-APPROVED DAILY DOSE OF FOOD?

Keeping your blood sugar level and your weight under control is facilitated by eating the proper amounts of meals. Help with determining daily caloric intake and portion sizes can be obtained from members of your healthcare team.

PLANNING FOR WEIGHT LOSS

Create a weight loss strategy with the help of your healthcare providers if you are overweight or obese.

The Body Weight Planner is a useful tool for creating personalized diet and exercise regimens that will get you to and keep you at your ideal weight.

Consuming fewer calories and switching to healthier options that are lower in fat and sugar will help you shed extra pounds.

If you are hoping to have a baby but are diabetic, overweight, or obese, losing weight before you get pregnant is a good idea.

MEAL PLAN METHODS

The plate technique and carbohydrate counting (commonly known as carb counting) are two popular strategies for helping people with diabetes plan how much food they will consume. Counting carbohydrates is the main topic of this book.

CHAPTER TWO

CARB COUNTING

People with diabetes can keep their blood sugar levels in check by organizing their meals around the number of carbohydrates (or "Carb Counting") they ingest at each meal. Carbohydrate counting has risen in significance as a means of controlling diabetes due to increased patient education and awareness. Improved glycemic control and quality of life for people with diabetes may result from adopting this strategy.

CC may have beneficial benefits on metabolic regulation, according to the available evidence.

Incorporating meal and snack planning into a child's or adolescent's routine can help them better control their Type 1 Diabetes.

- Assists in determining appropriate Insulin dosing.

- Decreases the occurrence of hypoglycemia.

- Reduces the concentration of glucose in the blood after a meal, which helps lower blood sugar levels and triglyceride levels (HbA1c).

- Enhances one's standard of living.

To begin, let's define carbohydrates.

Carbohydrates, or "carbs" as they're more affectionately known, are a type of sugar that may be found in foods including grains, fruits, dairy products, and desserts. Fruit (in any form), candies, baked products, and sugar itself are all included in this category. This also applies to all starchy foods, such as rice, potatoes, and pasta. The body metabolizes them into glucose, which is then utilized for energy. However, those who suffer from diabetes have problems metabolizing certain meals, and consuming too much of them can cause a dangerous rise in blood sugar.

Keep in mind that all foods, even green vegetables, include some carbohydrates and that many savory sauces are more sugar-based than you may anticipate.

Carbohydrates, which have the greatest effect on blood sugar levels, should be the primary focus of anyone with diabetes or a pre-diabetes diet.

IN WHAT WAYS DO CARBS VARY FROM ONE ANOTHER

Carbohydrates may be divided into three categories.

Sugars, whether they are the naturally occurring kind found in fruit and milk or the artificially added kind found in soda and many other processed meals.

Wheat, oats, and other grains, corn, potatoes, and other starchy vegetables, and dry beans, lentils, and peas are all examples of starches.

That component of plant foods that don't break down in the digestive process yet is beneficial to health is called fiber.

Blood sugar levels are increased by both sugars and carbohydrates, but not fiber.

HOW TO FIGURE OUT INSULIN DOSAGES?

GLYCAEMIC INDEX, INSULIN SENSITIVITY FACTOR, and INSULIN CARBOHYDRATE RATIO (GI)

Insulin sensitivity determines an individual's insulin-to-carbohydrate ratio (ICR), or the number of grams of carbs needed to cover 1 unit of insulin. Mealtime insulin requirements may be calculated using ICR by inputting information about the meal's carbohydrate content, the person's current blood glucose level, and plans for the rest of the day. For extremely young children who require fewer than 10 units of insulin per day, the 500 rule or the 300-450 rule, an empirical technique, is typically used to determine the carbohydrate-to-insulin ratio.

As an example,

A diabetic 25-year-old guy Height: 5'6" (168 cm)

Weight: 62 kg

22 kg/m2 BMI

ICR/CHO COVERAGE DOSE CALCULATION

There are two ways to calculate the insulin carbohydrate ratio or carbohydrate coverage dosage.

BY THE 450/500 RULE

THE CALCULATIONS BY BODY WEIGHT ARE AS FOLLOWS:

1. BY 450/500 RULE

500 rule for aspart, lispro, and glulisine users.

500 / Total Daily Insulin (Basal + Bolus) = 14.7 = 15 gram

1 insulin unit will cover about 15g of carbs.

The 450 Rule for Regular Insulin Users is 450/34 = 13.2 = 13gm, which means that 1 unit of insulin will cover roughly 13 gm of carbohydrates.

TOTAL DAILY INSULIN DOSE CALCULATING (TDI)

TDI = 0.55 X Weight in kg, resulting in 55 x 62.0 = 34 units of insulin per day.

BASAL AND BOLUS INSULIN DOSE CALCULATING

50% of TDI Equals bolus insulin dose

So, 50% of 34 units = 17 units to cover the entire CHO/day at mealtime 2. 2.8 X body weight (in pounds) / TDI BY BODY WEIGHT

So, 2.8 x (62.0 x 2.2) / TDI 2.8 x 136.4 lb / 34 = 11.2 gm, which means that 1 unit of insulin will cover about 11 gm of carbs.

INSULIN SENSITIVITY FACTOR (ISF)

The insulin sensitivity factor (ISF) is a pre-prandial glycemic adjustment method. ISF, specifically, reveals how much mmol/L (or mg/dL) blood glucose is reduced by 1 unit of insulin; it is calculated by dividing 1800 (rapid analog) or 1500 (normal insulin) by the TDD. ISF must also be tailored to each unique patient. ISF is usually greater in babies and toddlers, ranging between 100 and 150 mg/dL.

Correction Factor (CF) = 1500/TDI

So, 1800/34 = 52.9, or 1500/34 = 44.1.

As a result, one unit of insulin reduces blood glucose by 53 mg/dl. Difference between actual and goal blood glucose levels Factor of correction

As a result, the actual blood glucose level before breakfast is 226 mg/dl.

120 mg/dl is the target blood glucose level before breakfast.

Then,

226 - 120 / 53 = 2 units

As a result, the total dose before breakfast is equal to the CHO insulin dose plus 2 units.

THE GLYCAEMIC INDEX

The Glycemic Index, or GI, is another element to consider.

The GI measures the glycemic reaction to a known amount of carbs in meals in comparison to the same amount of carbohydrates in white bread. The glycemic area measured 90 minutes after eating is represented as The GI represents the glycemic reaction to a known amount of a percentage of the standard. Using the GI and eating low-GI foods may have little impact on postprandial hyperglycemia management. Furthermore, the notion of the glycaemic load was created to take into account both the quality and quantity of carbs.

A SAMPLE MENU

This sample dinner has around 1,800 calories, 200 grams of carbohydrates, and 13 carb portions.

BREAKFAST

12 cups oats, rolled (28g)

1 cup skim milk (13g)

a third of a medium banana (20g)

14 cups walnuts, chopped (4g)

65 grams total carbohydrates, or roughly 4 carb portions

LUNCH

2 whole wheat bread slices (24g)

4 oz. turkey meat (low sodium) (1g)

1 low-fat Swiss cheese slice (1g)

12 big tomatoes (3g)

1 tablespoon yellow mustard (1g)

14 cups chopped lettuce (0g)

8 small carrots (7g)

6 oz. fat-free plain Greek yogurt (7g)

a quarter cup of blueberries (15g)

Total carbs: 59 grams, or around 4 carb portions

DINNER

6 oz. roasted chicken breast (0g)

1 pound brown rice (45g)

1 cup broccoli, steaming (12g)

2 tablespoons margarine (0g)

Total carbs: 57 grams, or around 4 carb portions

SNACK

1 string cheese stick (low-fat) (1g)

two tangerines (18g)

Total carbs: 19 g (about 1 carb serving)

HOW TO CALCULATE CARBS

There are two types of carbohydrates: complex and simple. All carbohydrates are metabolized by the body into glucose or blood sugar. However, glucose levels might increase slowly with complex carbohydrates while they rise rapidly with simple carbohydrates. Foods like beans, peas, and whole grains, as well as fruits and vegetables, are good sources of complex carbohydrates. Many different forms of vitamins, minerals, and fiber may be found in foods that are rich in complex carbohydrates. Fruits, milk, dairy products, candies, syrups, soda, and any forms of processed or refined sugar are all examples of simple carbohydrates. Fruit, milk, and other dairy products are examples of simple carbohydrates that should be included in a balanced diet.

HELPFUL TIPS FOR READING FOOD LABELS

Learn what must be included on nutritional labels. All food items sold in the United States must comply with labeling regulations set by the Food and Drug Administration (FDA). To decipher food labels, one needs to know what information is required, where it must appear, and what each item means.

The "declaration of identification" and the net quantity or amount included in the package must be printed on the PDP, or primary display panel, of all food products. You can read this part of the label when the product is displayed on a shelf.

Although the brand name is also likely to appear on the PDP, the "statement of identification" is not to be confused with it. Names for products must accurately reflect their function (e.g. tomato soup, uncooked pasta, etc.).

Food labels in the United States must feature both metric and imperial measures.

Manufacturers of consumable foods are also required to label their goods with an "information panel" (IP). In the case of a package, the IP should be located on the panel or area directly to the right of the PDP. If the information was not included on the PDP, it must be included here, including the name and address of the maker, the name of the distributor, the ingredients, and nutritional and allergy information.

Decipher the list of ingredients. All components in a recipe should be listed by decreasing frequency and weight (i.e. the most abundant item is listed first). There should be a requirement for packaged goods to identify any additional water used in the process of packing as an ingredient. Furthermore, the names of ingredients should be those that are widely known (e.g. sugar instead of sucrose).

Any chemical preservatives used in the product must also be disclosed. In addition to the preservative's name, a brief explanation of the chemical's function (such as "Ascorbic Acid to Promote Color Retention") is required.

Realize the significance of allergy identification labels. What must be disclosed as allergens on a food label is outlined by the Food Allergen Labeling and Consumer Protection Act of 2004 (FALCPA)? The United States Department of Agriculture enforces strict labeling regulations for meat, poultry, and egg products (USDA). According to FALCPA, the top eight allergies are milk, eggs, fish, shellfish, tree nuts, wheat, peanuts, and soybeans. Approximately 90% of the cases of food allergy in the United States may be traced back to these foods. These "major" allergens are the only ones that have to be disclosed to consumers.

No FALCPA labeling is required for unprocessed agricultural products like fresh fruits and vegetables.

Crustacean shellfish like crab, lobster, shrimp, etc. are the only ones to which some people are allergic. Foods from the bivalve mollusk family, such as oysters, mussels, etc., do not trigger allergic reactions in most people.

Allergens must be mentioned in ingredient lists, but FALCPA requirements mandate that they be presented in a distinct, prominent manner (e.g. "Contains eggs, milk.").

Learn how to decipher food labels. All packaged goods must have nutritional information (except for alcohol and foods that meet certain requirements). On the other hand, the FDA does not mandate a specific method for determining these figures. This means that rather than relying on the precise amounts shown on the package, food producers can instead utilize "average" figures that are relevant to their product.

The FDA also does not verify the accuracy of manufacturers' nutrient counts, since it expects them to comply.

Keep in mind that not all items need a nutrition label. Products sold individually at the deli or bakery counter (unpackaged), most spices, fresh produce, and seafood, individual items packaged within a multi-pack (only the outer packaging requires a nutritional label), and food items given away and not for sale are exempt from the requirement for a label (although you can certainly ask for the information).

Calorie-free and 0 calories are allowed on packaging and nutrition labels for foods with less than 5 calories per serving.

As a general rule, you can round down to the closest 5-calorie increment for serving sizes of 50 calories or less. If there are more than 50 calories in an item, round up.

Nutritional labels don't have to list fat content if there's less than half a gram of fat per serving. Round to the closest half-gram for foods having a fat content between 0.5 and 5 grams. For items with a fat content of more than five grams, round up to the nearest whole gram.

Learn the meaning of "an excellent source of" and "high" when it comes to nutritional claims. The Product and Drug Administration (FDA) regulates the nutritional claims that can be made on food labels. If a claim is to be made on a product's packaging, it must first comply with the standards set out by each of these NCCs.

A product can be labeled as "an excellent source of" a nutrient (like fiber) if it provides 10-19% of the daily recommended intake of that nutrient (for example, "a good source of fiber" can be used if the product provides 15% of the daily recommended intake of fiber).

Consider a product "rich in fiber" if it provides more than 20% of your daily fiber needs "if it includes 25% of the recommended daily allowance of fiber.

Verify your knowledge of the meanings of "cheap," "light," and "free." Low-fat, fat-free, sugar-free, and similar descriptors fall under the umbrella term "nutrient content claims" (NCCs). For example, "minimal fat" or similar claims are not allowed to be made by manufacturers that have not been licensed by the FDA.

To avoid consumer confusion, producers cannot advertise non-specially processed items as "low" or "free" (such as "low in fat" for frozen peas) unless such items meet those standards.

Only items with a non-promoted "normal" version may use "free" and "low" claims. To qualify as a "low" or "free" version, the original product must have been altered in some way to include less of the targeted substance (such as fat, sugar, etc.) than the standard variant.

The percentage by which the food has been modified; the name of the reference food; and the quantity of the nutrient that is in both the labeled product and the reference food must all be included on the label when making a "light," "reduced," "less," "fewer," "more," or "added" claim. As an illustration, "50% fewer calories than xxx." Light xxx has 4g of fat per serving, whereas regular xxx has 8g."

Learn to identify "healthy" and "fresh" foods. The terms "healthy" and "fresh" can only be used on packaged goods that fulfill specific requirements, much like other NCCs.

To be considered "healthy," a product must meet all of the following criteria: it must be low in total fat, low in saturated fat, contain less than 480 milligrams of sodium (per standard serving), have cholesterol levels so low that they are not disclosed, and provide at least 10% of the daily recommended value of vitamin A, vitamin C, calcium, iron, protein, or fiber.

Fresh products are those that have not been frozen or preserved by other heat processes.

Check the percentage of daily value to see whether it's a good fit for you. There must be a table on the back of all packaged foods detailing the contents, including the various vitamins and minerals. Except in very specific cases, the table must include all nutrients. Also included in the table should be the percentage of the Recommended Daily Value the nutrient contributes per serving (RDVs). The RDVs are based on a 2,000-calorie diet, however. Keep in mind that the recommended daily allowance for a healthy adult is 2,050 calories. This is why these numbers should be seen as a rough estimate.

Learn the formula for determining carbohydrate content on food labels. The following formula is required by the FDA for manufacturers to determine the total carbs in their products. Glycemic Load = (Weight of Crude Protein + Weight of Total Fat + Weight of Moisture + Weight of Ash) x Weight of Food Serving. Carbohydrates like sugar and fiber need to be broken out on food labels.

In the case of foods with less than 1 gram of fiber and/or sugar, the expressions "less than 1 gram," "contains less than 1 gram," and "not a substantial source of dietary fiber/sugar" may be used by the maker. There's no need for them to figure out the precise amount.

HOW TO FIGURE OUT HOW MANY CARBS YOU'VE EATEN

Calculate the ideal percentage of carbohydrates in your diet. Most people do well with a diet that consists of 40-60% carbs. People with diabetes, polycystic ovary syndrome, and maybe other diseases may have reduced levels of this. Fruits, vegetables, dairy products, and grains are all good sources of carbohydrates, but meat is a poor source. On average, four calories may be extracted from a gram of carbohydrates.

Remember that carbohydrates are not the only thing you need to count and calculate as part of your diet, regardless of whether you count net carbs or total carbs. A balanced diet also includes fat and protein, which you should consume. Similarly, limiting your salt consumption is a good idea.

Make the carb count into a serving size for various foods. Carbohydrate intake can be limited by counting portions of fruits, vegetables, dairy products, and grains. Your age and gender will determine how many servings you need to consume daily.

The following ranges of daily servings are recommended for individuals of both sexes.

Aim for 5–8 servings of grains every day. One slice of bread, a cup of cereal, a half cup of rice, or a third of a cup of cooked pasta all count as grains. Whole grains should make up at least half of your daily grain intake.

Four to ten daily servings of fruits and vegetables. One-half cup of

100% fruit or vegetable juice, one big carrot, one cup of leafy greens, one medium apple, half a cup of berries, or twenty grapes all count as one serving of fruit or vegetable.

Two to three servings of dairy products daily. One serving of dairy products would consist of one cup of skim milk, half a cup of hard cheese, or three-quarters of a cup of yogurt.

If you want to acquire enough protein in your diet, you need to eat anywhere between one and three servings of meat or meat substitutes per day. Two eggs, two teaspoons of peanut butter, half a cup of lean meat, or three-quarters of a cup of tofu would all qualify as one serving.

Unsaturated fats are not specifically included in the dietary guidelines, but they are essential to a balanced diet and should be consumed daily. Two to three tablespoons are about right for the typical individual. Examples of foods high in unsaturated fats include vegetable oils, oil-based salad dressings, and soft, non-hydrogenated margarine.

Master the art of weighing your portions. The carbohydrate content of a food item, or the appropriate portion size, can also be determined by weighing the item in question. It's easy to get a kitchen scale at any store, and they're not too pricey.

You need to know the weight of the food item and the "factor" for that food item to calculate the grams of carbohydrates in your food depending on the weight.

Factors vary depending on the food category (e.g. bread has a factor of 15, which means there are 15 grams of carbs for every ounce of bread).

Take the case of wanting to know how many carbohydrates are in a dish of strawberries. Let's start with a weight for the strawberries. Suppose you weigh your supply of strawberries and find that you have 10 ounces. Second, 2.17 is the food value for strawberries if you're interested. For the third step, multiply the weight by the meal factor: 10 ounces x 2.17 Equals 21.7 grams of carbohydrates.

The number of servings in a food item may also be calculated by its weight. A half cup of meat or poultry is considered a serving size. This is around 75 grams (or 2.5 ounces). You can get 1.6 servings out of a 4-ounce piece of cooked chicken if you divide its weight by 2.5.

You should visually estimate how much food you will consume. Apples, oranges, bananas, eggs, and pieces of bread or bagels may all be roughly estimated just by looking at them. Cheese, pork, and other sliced or ground products that aren't packaged might be more challenging to gauge than other foods. When you're not at home or preparing the meal yourself, there are several visual aids available to assist you in determining how much food you should be eating.

For reference, a baseball-sized portion of dry cereal equals one cup.

A half cup of cooked cereal, rice, or pasta is about the size of a regulation baseball.

You can fit a tennis ball into the cavity of a single orange, apple, or pear.

A golf ball is about the size of a 1/4 cup of raisins.

One "medium" potato, when baked, is about the size of a computer mouse.

One cup of chopped veggies or salad mix is about the size of a baseball or a handful.

A 9-volt battery is around the size of a 50-gram portion of hard cheese, which is virtually the same thing (the rectangle ones).

A half-cup meal of lean beef or chicken will be about the size of a standard deck of playing cards.

A half-cup dish of grilled or baked fish will be around the size of a checkbook.

One teaspoon of margarine is about the size of a standard postage stamp, and there are three teaspoons in a tablespoon.

When it comes to oils and salad dressings, a single teaspoon seems like it would be enough to fill the top of a standard water bottle.

Find out how many carbohydrates are in the packaged goods you eat. You may get the total amount of carbohydrates in a packaged item by reading the nutritional label. But there are a handful of things you need to understand when utilizing these statistics to calculate how much carbohydrates you're eating.

The manufacturer-specified serving size was used to compile nutritional data. In certain circumstances, like an individual carton of yogurt, the serving size equals the actual quantity you're likely to consume. Cold cereal is one example of a food where a serving size is often substantially less than the typical bowl.

You will need to multiply the number of carbs per serving on the nutrition label by the number of servings you consume. For example, if the label for a cold cereal states there are 10 grams of carbohydrates per ½ cup of cereal, but you're intending to have 1 ½ cups of cereal, you will need to multiply 10 grams by 3 to get the actual carbs you'll be ingesting. For this specific case, let's use 30 grams.

Do not forget there are excellent carbohydrates. Nutritional labels will indicate Total Carbohydrates, Dietary Fibre, and Sugars. Dietary fiber and sugar are both carbohydrates, but your body doesn't utilize them in the same way. Fibre is not processed by your body, rather, your body just passes fiber all the way through. Constipation and intestinal health, in general, can benefit from fiber, as can lowering cholesterol, maintaining healthy blood sugar levels, and slimming down.

Men 50 or younger should eat 38 grams of fiber each day. Men over the age of 50 should aim for 30 grams each day.

If you are under the age of 50, you should consume 25 grams of fiber daily. Over 50 females should aim for 21 grams daily.

Keep in mind that fiber is a kind of carbohydrate, so you may include grams of fiber in your total carbohydrate count.

Learn how much carbohydrates you are now taking in. Keeping track of how many carbohydrates you eat each day can be useful in a variety of contexts when dieting. Knowing how many calories you consume daily can help you make informed decisions about how many calories to cut or add to your diet to achieve your weight loss or weight gain goals. Even if you have no intention of changing your weight, now is a good time to create a healthy eating plan that incorporates more nutritious sources of carbohydrates.

You might begin by keeping a notebook or making a spreadsheet on your computer.

The more specific you can be about what you consume on a daily (or even hourly) basis, the more likely you will be able to achieve your goals.

Keep tabs on yourself for a week, presuming that this week is representative of a typical one for you. Sauces, butter/margarine/dressings, etc., should also be included.

Write down the details from the food's nutritional label in your diary if you consume anything from a package.

It is a good idea to check the restaurants' websites before dining there to find nutritional information about the food. Get a brochure from your server if you'd like.

Calculate the daily totals for energy intake, carbohydrate intake, and fiber intake. Since your total diet plan will need to account for fat and protein, you should probably include these as well.

Use your figures as a starting point for building a future strategy. There are excellent applications available now for phones that allow consumers to track their daily consumption of all nutrients; carbs included.

STRATEGIC DIETARY CARBOHYDRATE PLANNING

Establish a target for yourself. Setting objectives is the first step in the planning process. Do you hope to keep your current weight but perhaps improve your diet? What are your weight-related goals? Your future calorie needs may be estimated using your present calorie intake as a baseline.

It's important to keep in mind that it requires a decrease of 500 calories per day (on average) to lose one pound each week.

Most individuals can do this by eating fewer carbs. Make sure you don't drastically reduce any macronutrients. Protein and healthy fat are essential for cell repair and hormone synthesis, so don't skimp on them too much.

Example: Let's pretend your daily calorie count is 2,000. You've calculated that reducing your calorie intake to 1,500 per day will help you lose weight healthfully. The majority of your daily caloric intake should come from carbohydrates (40-60%). Take it that you want half of your caloric intake to come from carbohydrates; it will make things a lot simpler. Your daily carb intake should be 50% of your total calorie intake or 750 calories. Now, divide your daily calorie total by 4 (there are 4 calories in every gram of carbohydrate) to arrive at your daily carbohydrate intake goal of 187.5 grams. Amounts of calories and carbohydrates for the day have been provided.

Prepare a menu for the week. Make a food plan based on your daily calorie and carbohydrate intake. You may calculate the calorie and carb content of the foods you eat by consulting the labels on the products you buy and the USDA's Super Tracker. With so much nutritional data at your fingertips, the Super Tracker is an excellent online planning tool.

In addition to monitoring your sleep and eating habits, the Super Tracker will serve as a daily workout reminder.

It's important to remember to get daily fiber. You should begin your day with a meal that contains at least 5 grams of fiber. Half of your daily grain intake should come from whole grains. Choose bread with 2 grams of fiber or more per slice (a bread serving is normally 1 slice). In place of refined white flour, try using whole wheat flour in your baked goods. Prepare soups and sauces by including fresh or frozen veggies. Vegetable soup and salad are better off with the addition of beans, peas, or lentils.

The fiber content of cereals can be improved by adding unrefined wheat bran.

As an alternative to "white" rice, try brown rice, wild rice, barley, whole wheat pasta, and bulgur.

Baking bread with whole wheat flour instead of white flour may require additional yeast or a longer rising time. One teaspoon of baking powder should be added for every three cups of whole grain flour in a recipe.

The convenient portability of many fruits makes them ideal fiber-rich snack options.

There is also a lot of fiber in nuts and dried fruit, albeit the sugar content varies widely across different varieties of dried fruit.

Beverage nutrients have to be considered as well. Your calorie count for the day will be affected by whatever you ingest, even gum. However, beverages could be the most disregarded. Water is the only beverage you can drink without worrying about your calorie intake. While black coffee or tea might not have many calories on its own, adding milk, cream, or sugar can quickly add up. The most common offender is sugary beverages. The calories in regular soda, energy drinks, juice, and sweetened beverages like tea and coffee may add up rapidly.

Try to keep in mind that drinking fruit juice is not the same as eating whole fruit. Despite having the same number of calories, juice and whole fruit are not interchangeable. Whole fruit contains fiber, which mitigates the rise in blood sugar levels that results from eating carbs. The low fiber content in juices leads to rapid glucose and insulin spikes. The entire fruit is preferable to the juice.

CARB COUNTING TOOLS

Despite our present cultural obsession with having everything on our phones, when it comes to rapid, convenient carb lookup, a basic printout of carb baselines stuck to the inside of your kitchen cabinet or a pocket-sized booklet kept in your glove box is hard to match.

Aside from a food database, the most important tool for calculating carbohydrates is a method for determining portion sizes. For liquids, a nice old-fashioned Pyrex measuring cup is ideal, and sets of smaller spoon-like nested measuring cups are ideal for measuring rice and pasta side dishes. Some individuals keep an additional set in the cabinet, besides these foods or their breakfast cereal, for easy mealtime measurement.

A nutrition scale, which is a step up in technology, provides a rapid and precise way to calculate portion size. Choose one with a "tare" feature, which allows you to zero out the scale with the weight of the plate or container on it, allowing you to simply weigh the food. Many nutrition scales are pre-programmed with data on hundreds of fresh fruits and vegetables, allowing you to weigh and calculate carbs in one step by simply inputting the code for the food you're weighing.

BEST CARB COUNTING APPS

While the "totally automated carb analyzer" app has yet to be created (darn it), there are an increasing number of applications that can help you better acquire, crunch, and manage carb-counting data.

Others are databases, some are tracking systems, and the majority are a combination of the two. Users give high grades to the following:

Foodvisor, which utilizes the camera on your smartphone to help you estimate portion size.

Daily Carb Pro is an app that allows you to create and track a "carb budget" for the day.

Carbohydrate Manager: The Keto Diet App is described as the world's most comprehensive carb counter, with over a million meals included.

My Fitness Pal is one of the world's most popular fitness applications, with a large food database and several monitoring features ranging from food consumption to step counting.

Atkins Carb & Meal Tracker, which includes a barcode zapper that quickly counts packaged carbohydrates.

Calorie King Food Search is a carb database with menu items from 260 national restaurant chains; for basic dishes, this app allows you to pick your portion size and does the arithmetic for you.

HOW MANY CARBS?

How many carbohydrates should you consume now that you know how to calculate them?

There is no one correct solution to this question. National dietary standards recommend 225-325 grams of carbohydrates per day, with 45 to 60 grams of carbs consumed every meal.

Low-carb regimens, such as the Atkins diet, restrict carbohydrates to 20-100 total carbs per day, or fewer than 30 grams each meal. It is entirely dependent on your age, health, weight, gender, and medicines. Inquire with your medical team about what is best for you.

Ironically, because they can "dose for it," PWDs who take mealtime insulin can potentially handle higher-carb meals better than PWDs who do not. With high-carb diets, blood sugars will be more variable, making diabetes control more challenging, but administering insulin gives an instant method to balance the sugar surge — which is more difficult with oral drugs.

Those who do not take insulin, on the other hand, will nearly always have raised blood sugar levels after eating — and the more carbohydrates consumed, the higher the post-meal sugar level.

Lower carbohydrate meals appear to be the trend in the most recent diabetic recommendations. While conceding that "carbohydrate consumption necessary for optimal health in humans is uncertain," the new ADA Consensus report goes on to highlight that lowering carbohydrates has "demonstrated the most evidence" for better blood glucose levels in PWDs. Lower carbohydrates, according to the ADA, can be "used in a range of dietary patterns."

MASTERING CARB COUNTING

So, what does it take to become a master at carb counting? All you need are the right tools and the discipline to utilize them regularly. It is, however, simple to make mistakes, so don't beat yourself up if you under or over-estimate at any particular meal. The objective is to keep records so you may learn how to manage that meal better the following time.

Of course, like anything else, carb counting can be taken to the next level by utilizing technology such as continuous glucose monitors (CGM) to gain a deeper understanding of the impact of various types of carbs — as well as taking into account eating times, frequencies, exercise, meal size, and other factors.

However, any degree of carb counting — apprentice, journeyman, or master — is preferable to none at all for all PWDs.

CARB CHOICES

STARCH

One carbohydrate choice is equal to 15 grams of carbohydrates.

CARB CHOICES

BREAD FOOD SERVING SIZE

Bagel - ¼ big bagel (1 oz.)

Biscuit - 1 biscuit (2½ inches across)

bread with fewer calories and less weight

- 2 slices (1½ oz.)

Cornbread - 1 and 14-inch cubes (112 ounces).

English muffin — a fraction of a muffin

Hot dog or hamburger bun - ½ bun (¾ oz.)

Chapati, naan, or roti — pick one!

1 oz.

Pancake

1 pancake (with a diameter of 4" and a thickness of 14")

Pita (6 inches across) (6 inches across)

½ pita

Tortilla, corn

1 small tortilla (6 inches across)

Tortilla, flour (white or whole-wheat)

1 small tortilla (with a diameter of 6 inches) or one-third of a large tortilla (10 inches across)

Waffle

1 waffle (4-inch square or 4 inches across)

CEREALS AND GRAINS* (INCLUDING PASTA AND RICE)

FOOD SERVING SIZE

Barley, couscous, millet, pasta (white or whole-wheat, all shapes and sizes), polenta, quinoa (all colors), or rice are some examples of grains that can be used here (white, brown, and other colors and types)

1/3 cup of twigs, buds, or flakes made from bran cereal, 1/3 cup plain shredded wheat, or 1/3 cup sugar-coated cereal

12 cup of bulgur, kasha, tabbouleh (also spelled tabouli), or wild rice

½ cup Granola cereal

¼ cup Hot cereal (oats, oatmeal, grits)

12 cup of ready-to-eat cereal that is unsweetened * 34 cup

Cooked foods are used to determine the serving sizes of all grains and pasta.

STARCHY VEGETABLES* FOOD SERVING SIZE

A third of a cup of cassava, dasheen, or plantain

Corn, green peas, a variety of veggies, or parsnips are other options.

½ cup Marinara, pasta, or spaghetti sauce

½ cup Mixed veggies (with corn or peas)

1 cup of cooked potatoes with the skins on

¼ large (3 oz.)

potatoes, deep-fried in French oil (oven-baked)

1 cup (2 oz) (2 oz.)

A mixture of mashed potatoes, milk, and butter.

½ cup

Winter squash, squash (acorn, butternut)

1 cup of yams or sweet potatoes, boiled and mashed 12 cups (312 ounces)

*The serving sizes for all starchy vegetables are measured based on the veggies after they have been cooked.

CRUMBLES AND OTHER SNACKS

FOOD SERVING SIZE

Crackers, specifically animal 8 crackers

Graham crackers, crackers

3 crackers (squares measuring 2.5 inches each).

Crackers, either of the saltine or circular butter-type variety, six crackers

Granola or snack bar

1 bar (¾ oz.)

Three cups of popcorn, popped

Pretzels

¾ oz.

Crispy rice cakes

2 cakes (4 inches across)

Baked snack chips and snacks (potato, pita)

About 8 chips (0.3 ounces) in total.

Snack chips, in their normal form (tortilla, potato)

Approximately 13 chips (1 oz.)

BEANS AND LENTILS

Size of a Food Serving

Toasted Baked Beans

A third of a cup of cooked or canned beans (black, garbanzo, kidney, lima, navy, pinto, or white), lentils (any color), or peas (black-eyed and split), drained and rinsed.

½ cup

FRUITS

1 carbohydrate option Equals 15 grams of carbs

PLEASE BE AWARE THAT THE LISTED WEIGHTS INCLUDE BOTH THE SKIN AND THE CORE AND THE SEEDS.

Size of a Food Serving

Applesauce, unsweetened

½ cup Banana

1 very little banana, approximately 4 inches in length (4 oz.)

Blueberries

¾ cup Dried fruits (blueberries, cherries, cranberries, mixed fruit, raisins)

2 Tbsp. Fruit, canned

½ cup

Whole fruit, of modest size (apple)

1 tiny fruit (4 oz.)

Whole fruit, of moderate size (nectarine, orange, pear, tangerine)

1 medium fruit (6 oz.)

Fruit juice, unsweetened

½ cup

Grapes

17 tiny grapes (3 oz.)

Melon, diced

1 cup of whole strawberries, measured out.

1¼ cup MILK AND MILK SUBSTITUTES

1 carbohydrate option Equals 12 grams of carbs

FOOD SERVING SIZE

Various types of milk (nonfat, 1%, 2%, and full)

1 cup

Rice drink, unsweetened and calorie-free

1 cup of yogurt (including Greek yogurt), either unsweetened or sweetened with an artificial

sweetener * 2/3 cup (6 ounces) of yogurt *

Because the number of carbohydrates included in yogurt can vary greatly, it is important to read the nutrition label before consuming it.

NON-STARCHY VEGETABLES

One serving is equal to five grams of carbohydrates in terms of the food's serving size.

Vegetables, cooked

½ cup of Vegetables, raw

1 cup Vegetable juice

Non-starchy vegetables include asparagus, beets, broccoli, carrots, cauliflower, eggplant, green beans, greens (collard, dandelion, mustard, purslane, and turnip), mushrooms, onions, pea pods, peppers, spinach, squash (summer, crookneck, and zucchini), and tomatoes. One-half cup of non-starchy vegetables is equal to one serving. Because they contain relatively few carbohydrates, certain vegetables, such as salad greens (lettuce, romaine, spinach, and arugula), are regarded as free meals.

SWEETS AND DESSERTS

1 carbohydrate option Equals 15 grams of carbs

FOOD SERVING SIZE

Brownie, miniature, unfrosted, 1 1/4 inches square, and 7/8 inches tall (about 1 oz.)

unfrosted cake measuring 2 inches square (about 1 oz.)

Hard candy, three separate pieces

Ice cream, standard 1/2 cup Sugar-free or sugar-and-fat-free pudding

Ice cream, usual (made with fat-free milk)

a half cup of cookie sandwiches filled with creme filling

2 little cookies (approximately 34 an ounce total)

2 CHOICES OF CARBOHYDRATES EQUATE TO 30 GRAMS OF CARBOHYDRATES IN ONE SERVING OF FOOD

Sweets, chocolate, whether milk or dark and candy

1¾ oz. Cupcake, frosted

1 miniature cupcake, or approximately 134 an ounce.

Glazed doughnut of the yeast variety

1 doughnut with a diameter of 3 34 inches (2 oz.)

45 grams of carbohydrates may be obtained from each of the three carbohydrate options.

Flan 2∕3 cup

Fruit cobbler ½ cup (3½ oz.)

a fruit pie that is manufactured professionally and has two crusts.

a sixth of an eight-inch pie

COMBINATIONS OF NUTRITION

1 CHOICE OF CARBOHYDRATES IS EQUAL TO 15 GRAMS OF CARBOHYDRATES IN ONE SERVING OF FOOD

Soup (tomato, cream, broth-types) (tomato, cream, broth-types)

1 cup (8 oz) (8 oz.)

Beef or other types of meat and veggies braised in a sauce.

1 cup (8 oz) (8 oz.)

A CARBOHYDRATE FOOD SERVING SIZE OF 30 GRAMS REQUIRES 2 CHOICES OF CARBOHYDRATES.

Entrees in the form of casseroles, such as tuna noodle casserole, lasagna, spaghetti and meatball casserole, chili with beans casserole, and macaroni and cheese casserole.

1 cup (8 oz) (8 oz.)

Pizza, thin-crust

1/4 of a pizza with a diameter of 12 inches (5 oz.)

Potato or macaroni/pasta salad

½ cup

3 OPTIONS FOR CARBOHYDRATES, EACH CONTAINING 45 GRAMS OF CARBOHYDRATE IN THE SERVING SIZE OF THE FOOD

Burrito (beef and bean) (beef and bean)

1 burrito (5 oz.)

Dinner-type wholesome food that may be frozen (includes dessert and is usually less than 400 calories) 1 meal (approximately 9-12 oz) (about 9-12 oz.)

FAST FOODS

1 CHOICE OF CARBOHYDRATES IS EQUAL TO 15 GRAMS OF **CARBOHYDRATES IN ONE SERVING OF FOOD**

Breaded and fried chicken breasts with breadcrumbs.

1 breast from a chicken (about 7 oz. with bone and skin)

Chicken nuggets or tenders

6 pieces (or around 3.5 ounces)

Served with stir-fried veggies and your choice of meat, fish, or poultry

1 cup (approximately 6 oz) (about 6 oz.)

Egg roll, meat

1 egg roll (about 3 oz.)

Taco, crunchy, stuffed with meat and cheese

1 tiny taco (about 3 oz.)

A CARBOHYDRATE FOOD SERVING SIZE OF 30 GRAMS REQUIRES 2 CHOICES OF CARBOHYDRATES.

Various types of breakfast sandwiches, biscuits, and English muffins (with egg, meat, and cheese)

1 sandwich Hamburger, normal

1 hamburger (312 ounces) served on a bun.

Noodles and veggies smothered in a brown sauce (chow mein, lo mein)

1 cup 3 carbohydrate options = 45 grams carbs.

FOOD SERVING SIZE

Chicken sandwich, grilled (with lettuce, tomato, and spread)

1 sandwich (approximately 7 and a half ounces total)

Pommes Frites

1 medium order (about 5 oz.)

Submarine sandwich

1 six-inch subwoofer

CHAPTER THREE

INTRODUCTION TO PLATE COUNTING METHOD

How Does One Use a Diabetes Plate?

The Diabetes Plate Method is best understood as a Portion Management Method, which is communicated through a straightforward pie chart that depicts the plate. Its purpose is to assist in the management and regulation of the size and ratio of portions of food, particularly from meals that are high in starch and carbohydrates, to prevent high blood glucose levels.

Dietitians in Sweden initially developed what is now known as the Diabetes Plate Method in the 1980s under the name Swedish Plate Method. Its primary purpose was to simplify and make more understandable the process of meal planning for diabetics. The Swedish Plate Method was adopted and upgraded in the 1990s to match the dietary guidelines of the American Diabetes Association and the Academy of Nutrition and

Dietetics. This was done to make the Swedish Plate Method more accessible to diabetics. Since then, the method has gained in popularity, displacing other techniques to become the primary means by which Diabetes Meal Planning is taught and becoming the dominant method overall.

The Diabetes Plate Method requires just a plate that is 23 centimeters in diameter and enables people with Type 2 Diabetes to prepare perfectly balanced meals that contain the appropriate proportions of vegetables, protein, and carbohydrates. The plate technique avoids the need for arduous carb counting, weighing, or measurement for those who do not use insulin. These individuals do not require insulin. Carbohydrate counting, however, will still be necessary for those who use insulin to calculate the appropriate amount of insulin to consume.

HOW CAN ONE MAKE THE MOST OUT OF THE DIABETES PLATE METHOD?

There are several compelling arguments in favor of the plate approach. It guarantees that the nutrient requirements of the human body are satisfied regularly and that a person can get the most out of the food that they eat. People who do not have diabetes are also able to utilize it in their day-to-day lives, even though it was designed specifically for diabetics. Because making changes and developing new healthy routines is very easy to achieve, it is beneficial for newcomers to do so early on in their journey. Several ailments, such as obesity and the challenges that result from it, may be avoided, along with a variety of other health problems, by avoiding overeating.

PLATE SIZE

The standard size for a dinner plate is nine inches; however, this can change based on your height, weight, gender, and the intensity of your daily activities. People who are taller and more physically active typically require more food, and a plate that is 12 inches in diameter can be sufficient for them. It is essential to pay close attention to the signs that your body is giving you that it is full while you are eating to prevent overeating.

HOW TO CREATE A HEALTHY PLATE IN FOUR STEPS

Step 1: Cover one-half of your plate with vegetables that do not contain starch.

Included in this category are vegetables such as bell peppers, broccoli, carrots, lettuce, mushrooms, onions, tomatoes, spinach, cabbage, cauliflower, cucumbers, and other green leafy vegetables. Steer clear of potatoes because of the starch they contain. This offers several health benefits, including fiber, vitamins, minerals, and phytonutrients.

Step 2: Cover one-quarter of the plate with a lean protein source, such as chicken, turkey, fish, eggs, Greek yogurt, beans, or lentils. As long as the cheese and cottage cheese in question was produced using low-fat milk, they are acceptable additions to this category. Tofu is another fantastic choice for vegetarians and vegans to consider adding to their diets. In addition to its many other health benefits, protein improves digestion, maintains hormonal equilibrium, prevents the breakdown of muscular tissue, and helps to decrease hunger.

Step 3: Cover the remaining one-fourth of your plate with nutritious carbohydrate options.

Because they include a greater quantity of fiber, vitamins, and minerals, starchy vegetables and healthy grains is recommended. Steer clear of refined carbs. Potatoes, Sweet Potatoes, Butternut Squash, Maize, Beans and Lentils, Brown or Wild Rice, Quinoa, Oatmeal, Healthy Grain Bread, Whole Grain Tortillas, and Barley are all examples of grains that should be included in a healthy diet.

The fourth step is to incorporate healthy fats and beverages that are calorie-free.

Olive oil, avocados, nuts, water, or tea can be consumed continually to keep yourself hydrated.

BENEFITS OF THE DIABETES PLATE METHOD

The advantages of following the plate diet are as follows.

It provides a nutritious meal that may be swiftly and easily consumed.

Not only does it govern what you eat, but it also affects how much of it you ingest.

It helps to keep blood sugar levels from fluctuating too much, which can be dangerous.

Integrates smoothly with new app features such as artificial intelligence food detection.

It is more tolerant and mild, which makes it easier for customers to transition into a new diet.

Because it is so straightforward to use and understand, it is an excellent tool for students just starting.

WHAT ARE SOME OF THE CONSTRAINTS THAT ARE PLACED ON THE PLATE METHOD?

Every wonderful object has the potential to have at least one minor defect. In the case of the plate approach, this is also the case. There are a few issues that arise while using the plate approach, and these issues are as follows:

It is not thorough because it does not include any information on how to season food or how much salt or sugar to use.

Because it is not customized for each individual, it does not take into account the fact that there may be certain days on which you require additional carbs or energy.

It can be challenging to account for vegetarian and vegan diets using the plate technique, which excludes a significant portion of the population.

The plate technique is not the best solution for everyone, especially considering that some of these problems can be remedied by consulting with a nutritionist or dietician. When adhering to any diet, it is essential to keep one's unique requirements in mind.

BOTTOMLINE

The Plate Strategy is best described as a method of portion management based on a simple pie chart depicting the plate; its goal is to help control and regulate the size and ratio of portions of food from starchy, carbohydrate-rich meals to avoid excessive blood glucose levels. The Plate Strategy is best described as a method of portion management based on a simple pie chart depicting the plate; its goal is to help control and regulate the size and ratio of portions of food The size of the plate that you should use is 9 inches, however, this might change based on your height, weight, and the intensity of your activities. Pay close attention to the signs that your body is giving you that it is full while you are eating to prevent overeating. The plate diet recommends using a plate that is 9 inches in diameter since it has 44% less surface area than a standard plate. A diet that is mostly determined by the size of the plate that you eat off of is known as a diet that is "plate based." Dishes prepared using the plate approach could not satisfy the nutritional requirements of everyone. Because it is not customized to each individual, it does not take into account the possibility that there may be days on which you require additional carbs or energy.

FAQS

How exactly does one go about utilizing the Plate Method?

If you want to employ the plate approach, all you need is a plate and the food that you've just finished preparing. You should fill up half of your plate with vegetables that do not contain starch, one-quarter of the plate with meals high in protein, and the remaining quarter of the plate with foods high in carbohydrates and fiber. This will guarantee that you have sufficient amounts of all of the essential nutrients.

Does the Plate Method yield the desired results?

In a sense, this is correct. People like to load their plates up with food and then consume all that is there, therefore larger plates lead to greater consumption of calories, which in turn may lead to weight gain. The plate diet recommends utilizing a 9-inch plate rather than a 12-inch plate since the former has 44% less surface area than the latter, which will enable you to consume fewer calories and assist in the process of weight loss.

Is there any truth to the Plate Method?

People who suffer from diabetes have found that using plates to measure their food is quite helpful. It makes certain that kids receive the recommended amount of nutrients daily and aids in the management of their blood sugar levels. It is an excellent method for maintaining proper portion control and avoiding issues such as overeating, which can lead to obesity.

What exactly is a diet based on plates?

A diet that is mostly determined by the size of the plate that you eat off of is known as a diet that is "plate based." The size of the plate is taken into account when calculating the quantity of protein, carbs, and other food categories that should be consumed to keep a balanced diet and stable blood sugar levels. Dishes prepared using the plate approach could not satisfy the nutritional requirements of everyone.

THE END